Conversation:

What to Say and How to Say it

By

Mary Greer Conklin

CHAPTER I

INTRODUCTORY

WHAT CONVERSATION IS AND WHAT IT IS NOT

Good conversation is more easily defined by what it is not than by what it is. To come to any conclusions on this subject, one should first determine: What is the aim of conversation? Should the intention be to make intercourse with our fellows a free school in which to acquire information; should it be to disseminate knowledge; or should the object be to divert and to amuse? It might seem that any person with a good subject must talk well and be interesting. Alas! highly cultivated people are sometimes the most silent. Or, if they talk well, they are likely to talk *too* well to be good conversationalists, as did Coleridge and Macaulay, who talked long and hard about interesting subjects, but were nevertheless recorded as bores in conversation because they talked *at* people instead of talking *with* them. In society Browning was delightful in his talk. He would not discuss poetry, and was as communicative on the subject of a sandwich or the adventures of some woman's train at the last drawing-room as on more weighty subjects. Tho to some he may have seemed obscure in his art, all agreed that he was simple and natural in his discourse. Whatever he talked about, there could not be a moment's doubt as to his meaning.

From these facts concerning three men of genius, it can be inferred that we do not go into society to get instruction gratis; that good conversation is not necessarily a vehicle of information; that to be natural, easy, gay, is the catechism of good talk. No matter how learned a man is, he is often thrown with ordinary mortals; and the ordinary mortals have as much right to talk as the extraordinary ones. One can conceive, on the other hand, that when geniuses have leisure to mix in society their desire is to escape from the questions which daily burden their minds. If they prefer to confine themselves to an interchange of ideas apart from their special work, they have a right to do so. In this shrinking of people of genius from discussing the very subjects with regard to which their opinion is most valuable, there is no doubt a great loss to the world. But unless they themselves bring forth the topic of their art, it must remain in abeyance. Society has no right to force their mentioning it. This leads us, then, to the conclusion that the aim of conversation is to distract, to interest, to amuse; not to teach nor to be taught, unless incidentally. In good conversation people give their charm, their gaiety, their humor, certainly—and their wisdom, if they will. But conversation which essentially entertains is not essentially nonsense. Some one has drawn this subtle distinction: "I enter a room full of pleasant people as I go to see a picture, or listen to a song, or as I dance—that I may amuse myself, and invigorate myself, and raise my natural spirits, and laugh dull care away. True, there must be ideas, as in all amusements worthy of the name there is a certain seriousness impossible to define; only they must be kept in the background."

The aim and design of conversation is, therefore, pleasure. This agreed, we can determine its elements. Conversation, above all, is dialog, not monolog. It is a partnership, not an individual affair. It is listening as well as talking. Monopolizing tyrants of society who will allow no dog to bark in their presence are not conversationalists; they are lecturers. There are plenty of people who, as Mr. Benson says, "possess every qualification for conversing except the power to converse." There are plenty of people who deliver one monolog after another and call their talk conversation. The good conversationalists are not the ones who dominate the talk in any gathering. They are the people who have the grace to contribute something of their own while generously drawing out the best that is in others. They hazard topics for discussion and endeavor each to give to the other the chance of enlarging upon them. Conversation is the interchange of ideas; it is the willingness to communicate thought on all subjects, personal and universal, and in turn to listen to the sentiments of others regarding the ideas advanced.

Good conversation is the nimbleness of mind to take the chance word or the accidental subject and play upon it, and make it pass from guest to guest at dinner or in the drawing-room. It is the discussion of any topic whatever, from religion to the fashions, and the avoidance of any phase of any subject which might stir the irascible talker to controversy. As exprest by Cowper in his essay, "Conversation":

> "Ye powers who rule the tongue, if such there are,

> And make colloquial happiness your care,
> Preserve me from the thing I dread and hate—
> A duel in the form of a debate."

Wearing one's heart on one's sleeve is good for one conversationally. Ready conversers are people who give their thought to others in abundance; who make others feel a familiar heartbeat. No one can approach so near to us as the sincere talker, with his sympathy and his willing utterances. Luther, who stands out as one of the giants of the Renaissance, came into close human touch with his friends in talk; in conversation with him they could always feel his fierce and steady pulse.

Another element of successful conversation is good-humored tolerance, the willingness to bear rubs unavoidably occasioned. The talker who cavils at anything that is said stops conversation more than if he answered only yes or no to all remarks addrest to him. Still another element of good conversation is the right sort of gossip; gossip which is contemporary and past history of people we know and of people we don't know; gossip which is in no way a temptation to detract. Raillery may also become a legitimate part of good conversation, if the ridicule is like a good parody of good literature—in no way malignant or commonplace. "Shop," if nicely adjusted to the conversational conditions, may have its rightful share in interesting talk. Friends often meet together just to talk things over, to get each other's point of view, to hear each other tell of his own affairs, of his work and of his progress. "Shop" talk was sometimes the essence of those famous conversations of the seventeenth century coffee-house. Anecdotes are a natural part of conversation, but they become the bane of talk unless kept in strict restraint.

There are times when good conversation is momentary silence rather than speech. It is only the haranguers who feel it their duty to break in with idle and insincere chatter upon a pleasant and natural pause. A part of the good fellowship of acceptable conversation is what one might call "interest questions." "Interest questions" are just what the words imply, and have about them no suspicion of the inquisitive and impertinent catechizing which only fools, and not even knaves, indulge in.

The negative phase of conversation may largely grow out of a discussion of the positive. By discovering what conversation is, we find, in a measure, what it is not. It is not monolog nor monopolizing; it is not lecturing nor haranguing; it is not detracting gossip; it is not ill-timed "shop" talk; it is not controversy nor debate; it is not stringing anecdotes together; it is not inquisitive nor impertinent questioning. There are still other things which conversation is not: It is not cross-examining nor bullying; it is not over-emphatic, nor is it too insistent, nor doggedly domineering, talk. Nor is good conversation grumbling talk. No one can play to advantage the conversational game of toss and catch with a partner who is continually pelting him with grievances. It is out of the question to expect everybody, whether stranger or intimate, to choke in congenial sympathy with petty woes. The trivial and perverse annoyances of one's own life are compensating subjects for conversation only when they lead to a discussion of the phase of character or the fling of fate on which such-and-such incidents throw light, because the trend of the thought then encourages a tossing back of ideas.

Perhaps the most important thing which good conversation is not, is this: It is not talking for effect, or hedging. There are two kinds of hedging in conversation: one which comes from failing to follow the trend of the discussion; another which is the result of talking at random merely to make bulk. The first is tolerable; the last is contemptible. The moment one begins to talk for effect, or to hedge flippantly, he is talking insincerely. And when a good converser runs against this sort of talker, his heart calls out, with Carlyle, for an empty room, his tobacco, and his pipe. It is maintained by some one that there are three kinds of a bore: the person who tells the plot of a play, the one who tells the story of a novel, and the one who tells his dreams. This may be going too far with regard to dreams; for dreams, if handled in the right way, are easily made a part of interesting talk. But in sophisticated society books and plays are discust only by talking about the prevailing idea round which the story centers. They are criticized, not outlined. The most learned and cultivated talkers do not attempt the difficult and unrewarded feat of giving a concise summary of plots.

Good conversation, then, is the give and take of talk. A person who converses well also listens well. The one is inseparable from the other. Anything can be talked about in cultivated society provided the subjects are handled with humanity and discrimination. Even the weather and the three dreadful D's of conversation, Dress, Disease, and Domestics, may be made an acceptable part of talk if suited to the time, the place, and the situation. Nor is genius or scholarship essential to good conversation. The qualities most needed are tact, a sincere desire to please, and an appreciation of the truth that the man who never says a foolish thing in conversation will never say a wise one.

CHAPTER II

DISCUSSION *VERSUS* CONTROVERSY

Many people object to discussion, but they are invariably those on the midway rounds of the conversational ladder; people to whom the joy of the amicable intellectual tussle is unknown, and to whom the highest standards of the art of talking do not appeal. Where there is much intellectual activity discussion is sure to arise, for the simple reason that people will not think alike. Polite discussion is the most difficult and the most happy attainment of society as it is of literature; and why should oral discussion be less attractive than written? Dr. Johnson used to express unbounded contempt for all talk that was not discussion; and Robert Louis Stevenson has given us frankly his view: "There is a certain attitude, combative at once and deferential, eager to fight yet most averse to quarrel, which marks out at once the talkable man. It is not eloquence, nor fairness, nor obstinacy, but a certain proportion of all these that I love to encounter in my amicable adversaries. They must not be pontiffs holding doctrine, but huntsmen questing after elements of truth. Neither must they be boys to be instructed, but fellow-students with whom I may argue on equal terms." From Mr. John B. Yeats, one of the many Irishmen who have written tellingly on this interesting subject of human intercourse, we have: "Conversation is an art, as literature is, as painting is, as poetry is, and subject to the same laws from which nothing human is excluded, not even argument. There is literature which argues, and painting which argues, and poetry which argues, so why not conversation which argues? Only argument is the most difficult to mold into the most blessed shape of art."

Some people conceive an everlasting opposition between politeness and earnest discussion. Politeness consists, they think, in always saying, "yes, yes," or at most a non-committal "indeed?" to every word addrest to them. This is apt to be our American vice of conversation, where, for lack of courage in taking up discussion, talk often falls into a series of anecdotes. In Germany the tendency is to be swept away in discussion to the point of a verbal dispute.

There is no greater bore in society than the person who agrees with everybody. Discussion is the arena in which we measure the strength of one another's minds and run a friendly tilt in pleasing self-assertiveness; it is the common meeting-ground where it is understood that Barnabas will take gentle reproof from Paul, and Paul take gentle reproof from Barnabas. Those who look upon any dissent from their views as a personal affront to be visited with signs of resentment are no more fit for brilliant talk than they are fit for life and its vicissitudes. "Whoso keepeth his mouth and his tongue keepeth his soul in peace," it is true; but he also keeps himself dead to all human intercourse and as colorless in the world as an oyster. "Too great a desire to please," says Stevenson, "banishes from conversation all that is sterling.... It is better to emit a scream in the shape of a theory than to be entirely insensible to the jars and incongruities of life and take everything as it comes in a forlorn stupidity." This is equivalent to telling the individual who treads too nicely and fears a shock that he had pleased us better had he pleased us less, which is the subtle observation of Mr. Price Collier writing in the *North American Review*: "It is perhaps more often true of women than of men that they conceive affability as a concession. At any rate, it is not unusual to find a hostess busying herself with attempts to agree with all that is said, with the idea that she is thereby doing homage to the effeminate categorical imperative of etiquette, when in reality nothing becomes more quickly tiresome than incessant affirmatives, no matter how pleasantly they are modulated. Nor can one avoid one of two conclusions when one's talk is thus negligently agreed to: either the speaker is confining herself entirely to incontradictable platitudes, or the listener has no mind of her own; and in either case silence were golden. In this connection it were well to recall the really brilliant epigram of the Abbé de Saint-Réal, that 'On s'ennuie presque toujours avec ceux que l'on ennuie.' For not even a lover can fail to be bored at last by the constant lassitude of assent expressing itself in twin sentiments to his own. 'Coquetting with an echo,' Carlyle called it. For, tho it may make a man feel mentally masterful at first, it makes him feel mentally maudlin at last; and, as the Abbé says, to be bored one's self is a sure sign that one's companion is also weary."

Tho polite dissent is desirable in discussion, flat contradiction is contemptible. Dean Swift affirms that a person given to contradiction is more fit for Bedlam than for conversation. In discussion, far more than in lighter talk, decency as well as honor commands that each partner to the conversational game conform to the niceties and fairness of it. "I don't think so," "It isn't so," "I don't agree with you at all," are too flat and positive for true delicacy and refinement in conversation. "I have been inclined to think otherwise," "I should be pleased to hear your reasons," "Aren't you mistaken?" are more acceptable phrases with which to introduce dissent. In French society a discrepancy of views is always manifested by some courtesy-phrase, such as "*Mais, ne pensez-vous pas*" or "*Je vous demande pardon*"—the urbane substitutes for "No, you are wrong," "No, it isn't." Our own Benjamin Franklin, whose appreciation of the conversational art in France won completely the hearts of the French people, tells us in his autobiography that in later life he found it necessary to throw off habits acquired in youth: "I continued this positive method for some years, but gradually left it, retaining only the habit of expressing myself in terms of modest diffidence: never using when I advanced anything that might possibly be disputed, the words 'certainly,' 'undoubtedly,' or any others that give the air of positiveness to an opinion, but rather say, 'it appears to me,' or 'I should think it so-and-so, for such-and-such a reason,' or 'I imagine it to be so,' or it is so 'if I am not mistaken.'"

Unyielding obstinacy in discussion is deadening to conversation, and yet the extreme contrary is crippling. Open resentment of any attempt at warmth of speech is paralysis and torpor to talk. When one meets a hostess, or a conversational partner, "whose only pleasure is to be displeased," one is reminded of the railway superintendent who kept the wires hot with fault-finding messages bearing his initials "H. F. C." until he came to be known along the road as "Hell For Certain." People of a resentful turn of mind, whose every sentence is a wager, and who convert every word into a missile, are fit for polemical squabbles, but not for polite discussion. Those raucous persons who, when their opponents attempt to speak, cry out against it as a monstrous unfairness, are very well adapted to association with Kilkenny cats, but not with human beings. It is in order to vanquish by this means one who might otherwise outmatch them entirely that they thus seek to reduce their opponent to a mere interjection. "A man of culture," says Mr. Robert Waters, "is not intolerant of opposition. He frankly states his views on any given subject, without hesitating to say wherein he is ignorant or doubtful, and he is ready for correction and enlightenment wherever he finds it." Such a man never presses his hearers to accept his views; he not only tolerates but considers opposed opinions and listens attentively and respectfully to them. Hazlitt said of the charming discussion of Northcote, the painter: "He lends an ear to an observation as if you had brought him a piece of news, and enters into it with as much avidity and earnestness as if it interested only himself personally."

Of all the tenets of good conversation to which the French give heed, their devotion to listening is the most notable. From this judiciously receptive attitude springs their uninterrupting shrug of assent or disapproval. But listening is only one of their many established conversational dicta: "The conversation of Parisians is neither dissertation nor epigram; they have pleasantry without buffoonery; they associate with skill, with genius, and with reason, maxims and flashes of wit, sharp satire, and severe ethics. They run through all subjects that each may have something to say; they exhaust no subject for fear of tiring their hearer; they propose their themes casually and they treat them rapidly; each succeeding subject grows naturally out of the preceding one; each talker delivers his opinion and supports it briefly; no one attacks with undue heat the supposition of another, nor defends obstinately his own; they examine in order to enlighten, and stop before the discussion becomes a dispute." Such was Rousseau's description of Parisian conversation; and some one else has declared that the French are the only nation in the world who understand a *salon* whether in upholstery or talk. "Every Britisher," said Novalis more than a hundred years ago, "is an island"; and Heine once defined silence as "a conversation with Englishmen." We Americans, tho not so reserved in talk as our English brothers, are less respectful to conversational amenities; and both of us are far behind the French in the gracious art of verbal expression. Not only is the spoken English of the cultured Irish the most cosmopolitan and best modulated of any English in the world, but the conversation of cultivated Irishmen more adequately approaches the perfection of the French.

It is as illuminating to study the best models in human intercourse as to study the best models in literature, or painting, or any other art. One of the distinct elements in French conversation is that it is invariably kept general; and by general I mean including in the talk all the conversational group as opposed to *tête-à-tête* dialog. Many people disagree with the French in this. Addison declared that there is no such thing as conversation except between two persons; and Ralph Waldo Emerson and Walter Savage Landor said something of the same sort. Shelley was distinctly a *tête-à-tête* talker, as Mr. Benson, the present-day essayist, in some of his intimate discourses, proclaims himself to be. But Burke and Browning, the best conversationalists in the history of the Anglo-Saxon race, like all the famous women of the French *salon*, from Mme. Roland to Mme. de Staël, kept pace with any number of interlocutors on any number of subjects, from the most abstruse science to the lightest *jeu d'esprit*. Good talk between two is no doubt a duet of exquisite sympathy; but true conversation is more like a fugue in four or eight parts than like a duet. Furthermore, general and *tête-à-tête* conversation have both their place and occasion. At a dinner-table in France private chats are very quickly dispelled by some thoughtful moderator. Dinner guests who devote themselves to each other alone are not tolerated by the French hostess as by the English and American. Because *tête-à-tête* conversation is considered good form so generally among English-speaking peoples, I have in other essays adapted my comments on this subject to our customs; but talk which is distributed among several who conform to the courtesies and laws of good conversation is the best kind of talk. In general talk every one ought to have a voice. It is the undue humility of some and the arrogance and polemical tendency of others that prevent good general conversation. People have only to begin with three axioms: the first, that everybody is entitled, and often bound, to form his own opinion; second, that everybody is equally entitled to express that opinion; and third, that everybody's opinion is entitled to a hearing and to consideration, not only on the ground of courtesy, but because any opinion honestly and independently formed is worth something and contributes to the discussion.

Another principle of French conversation is that it is kept personal, in the sense, I mean, that the personality of the speakers suffuses it. "The theme being taken," as Stevenson says, "each talker plays on himself as on an instrument, affirming and justifying himself." This counter-assertion of personality, to all appearances, is combat, but at bottom is amicable. An issue which is essentially general and impersonal is lost in the accidental conflicts of personalities, because the quality which plays the most important part is presence of mind, not correct reasoning. A conversationalist whose argument is wholly fallacious will often, by exercise of verbal adroitness, dispose of an objection which is really fatal. The full swing of the personalities of the speakers in a conversation is what makes the flint strike fire. It is only from heated minds that the true essence of conversation springs; and it is in talk which glances from one to another of a group, more than in dialog, that this personality is reflected. "It is curious to note," says an editorial in *The Spectator*, "how very much dialog there is in the world, and how little true conversation; how very little, that is, of the genuine attempt to compare the different bearing of the same subject on the minds of different people. It is the rarest thing in the world to come, even in the best authors, on a successful picture of the different views taken by different minds on the same subject, and the grounds of the difference."

Quite as noticeable an element in French conversation is the attitude of the conversers to their subject. They never try to settle matters as if their decisions were the last court of appeal, and as if they must make frantic effort to carry their side of the question to victory. They discuss for the pleasure of discussing; not for the pleasure of vanquishing, nor even of convincing. They discuss, merely; they do not debate, nor do they enter into controversy.

One of the greatest conversational charms of the French is their amenity in leading talk. This grows out of a universal eagerness in France to take pains in conversation and to learn its unwritten behests. The uninitiated suspect little of the insight and care which matures even the natural conversational ability of a Madame de Staël or a Francisque Sarcey. The initiated know that the same principles which make the French prodigious conversationalists make them capable and charming hosts and hostesses. The talker who can follow in conversation knows how to lead, and vice versa. Without a leader or "moderator," as the admirable Scotch word has it, conversation is apt to become either tepid or demoralized; and often, for the want of proper and sophisticated leading, discussion that would otherwise be brilliant deteriorates into pandemonium. As paradoxical as it sounds on first thought, it is nevertheless true that thoroughly good conversation is impossible where there is too much talk. Some sort of order must be imperceptibly if not unconsciously maintained, or the sentences clash in general conversation. Leading conversation is the adroit speech which checks the refractory conversationalist and changes imperceptibly the subject when it is sufficiently threshed or grows over-heated; it is guiding the talk without palpable break into fresh fields of thought; it is the tact with which, unperceived, the too slow narration of a guest is hurried by such courteous interpolations as "So you got to the inn, and what then?" or, "Did the marriage take place after all?"; it is the art with which the skilful host or hostess sees that all are drawn into the conversational group; it is the watchfulness that sends the shuttle of talk in all directions instead of allowing it to rebound between a few; it is the interest with which a host or hostess solicits the opinions of guests, and develops whatever their answers may vaguely suggest; it is the care with which an accidentally interrupted speech of a guest is resuscitated; it is the consideration which puts one who arrives late in touch with the subject which was being discust just before his appearance. It is this concern for conversational cues which gives any host or hostess an almost unbounded power in social intercourse; for he is the best talker who can lead others to talk well.

It goes without saying that a people who have assimilated all the foregoing tenets of good conversation are never disjointed in their talk. Their consummate art of listening is responsible for their skill in following the logical trend of the discourse. This may be considered a national trait. In decent French society there are no abrupt transitions of thought in the different speeches. The speech of each speaker grows naturally out of what some one of his conversational partners has just been saying, or it is duly prefaced by an introductory sentence connecting it with a certain preceding speech. They know that, once embarked, no converser can tell where the give and take of talk will carry him; but they also know that this does not necessitate awkward and direct changes of subject. The weakness of inattention and of unconscious shunting in conversation is virtually unknown in good society in France.

Is it any wonder that in a country where conversation is considered an art capable of cultivation and having certain fixt principles, so many French women of humble birth, like Sophie Arnould and Julie Lespinasse, have earned their way to fame by their conversational powers? Is it any wonder that in France polite discussion is made the most exhilarating and delightful exercise in the world?

One reason there is so little acceptable conversational discussion is the indisposition of people in society to say what they think; their unwillingness to express their whole minds on any one subject. It is this element of unfettered expression or revelation which makes literature entertaining; why then withhold thought too cautiously from conversation? The habit of evasion is cowardly as well as unsocial; and nothing so augments conversation as being pleasantly downright; letting people know where to find you. The most preposterous views get respect if uttered intrepidly. Sincere speech is necessary to good conversation of any kind, and especially is it essential to discussion. One of the stupidest of conversational sins is quibbling—talking insincerely, just for the sake of using words, and shifting the point at issue to some incidental, subordinate argument on which the decision does not at all depend. It is the intellectually honest person who sparkles in discussion.

Another reason why discussion is waning is the disrespect we feel for great subjects. We only mention them, or hint at them; and this cannot lead to very brilliant talk. Tho prattle and persiflage have their place in conversation, talkers of the highest order tire of continually encouraging chit-chat. "What a piece of business; monstrous! I have not read it; impossible to get a box at the opera for another fortnight; how do you like my dress? It was immensely admired yesterday at the B——s; how badly your cravat is tied! Did you know that —— lost heavily by the crash of Thursday? That dear man's death gave me a good fit of crying; do you travel this summer? Is Blank really a man of genius? It is incomprehensible; they married only two years ago." This sort of nimble talk is all very well; but because one likes sillibub occasionally is no proof that one is willing to discard meat entirely. Conversational topics can be too trivial for recreation as well as too serious; and even important subjects can be handled in a light way if necessary. "Clever people are the best encyclopedias," said Goethe; and the great premier Gladstone was a charming man in society, though he never talked on any but serious subjects. He was noted for his ability to pump people dry without seeming in the least to probe. "True conversation is not content with thrust and parry, with mere sword-play of any kind, but should lay mind to mind and show the real lines of agreement and the real lines of divergence. Yet this is the very kind of conversation which seems to me so very rare." In order that a great subject shall be a good topic of conversation, it must provoke an enthusiasm of belief or disbelief; people must have decided opinions one way or the other. I believe with Stevenson that theology, of all subjects, is a suitable topic for conversational discussion, and for the reason he gives: that religion is the medium through which all the world considers life, and the dialect in which people express their judgments. Try to talk for any length of time with people to whom you must not mention creeds, morals, politics, or any other vital interest in life, and see how inane and fettered talk becomes.

The tranquil and yet spirited discussion of great subjects is the most stimulating of all talk. The thing to be desired is not the avoidance of discussion but the encouragement of it according to its unwritten codes and precepts. "The first condition of any conversation at all," says Professor Mahaffy of Dublin, "is that people should have their minds so far in sympathy that they are willing to talk upon the same subject, and to hear what each member of the company thinks about it. The higher condition which now comes before us is, that the speaker, apart from the matter of the conversation, feels an interest in his hearers as distinct persons, whose opinions and feelings he desires to know…. Sympathy, however, should not be excessive in quality, which makes it demonstrative. We have an excellent word which describes the over-sympathetic person, and marks the judgment of society, when we say that he or she is *gushing*. To be too sympathetic makes discussion, which implies difference of opinion, impossible." Those who try to discover how far conversation is advanced by sympathy and hindered by over-sympathy; those who attempt to detect to what extent wholesome discussion is degraded by acrid controversy, need not be afraid of vigorous intellectual buffeting. Discussion springs from human nature when it is under the influence of strong feeling, and is as much an ingredient of conversation as the vocalizing of sounds is a part of the effort of expressing thought.

CHAPTER III

GOSSIP

It seems strange that, in all the long list of brilliant dissertations on every subject under the sun, no English essayist should have yielded a word under the seductive title of "Gossip." Even Leigh Hunt, who wrote vivaciously and exquisitely on so many light topics, was not attracted by the enticing possibilities of this subject to which both the learned and the unlearned are ready at all times to bestow a willing ear or eye. One usually conceives gossip as something to which one lends only one's ear, and never one's eye; but what are "Plutarch's Lives" but the right sort of gossip? That so many literary men and women have vaguely suspected the alluring tone-color of the word "gossip" is proved by: *A Gossip in Romance*, Robert Louis Stevenson; *Gossip in a Library*, Edmund William Gosse; *Gossip of the Caribbees*, William R. H. Trowbridge, Jr.; *Gossip from Paris During the Second Empire*, Anthony North Peet; *Gossip in the First Decade of Victoria's Reign*, Jane West; *Gossip of the Century*, Julia Clara Byrne; *Gossiping Guide to Wales*, Askew Roberts and Edward Woodall; *Gossip with Girls and Maidens Betrothed and Free*, Blanche St. John Bellairs. Yet no one has ever thought of writing about gossip for its own sweet sake.

Among every-day words perhaps the word "gossip" is more to be reckoned with than any other in our language. The child who runs confidingly to mother to report his grievance is a gossip; he is also an historian. Certainly gossip is in its tone familiar and personal; it is the familiar and personal touch which makes *Plutarch's Lives* interesting. At the root of the word "gossip," say etymologists, there lies an honest Saxon meaning, "God's sib"—"of one kindred under God."

It would be only a misanthrope who would assert that he has no interest in his fellows. He is invariably a selfish person who shuns personality in talk and refuses to know anything about people; who says: "What is it to me whether this person has heard Slezak in *Tannhäuser*; what do I care whether Mrs. So-and-So has visited the French play; what concern is it of mine if Mr. Millions of eighty marries Miss Beautiful of eighteen; what is it to me whether you have watched the agonies of a furnishing party at Marshall Field's and have observed the bridegroom of tender years victimized by his wife and mother-in-law with their appeals to his excellent taste; of what interest to me are the accounts of the dissolute excesses which interspersed the wild outbreaks of religious fanaticism of Henry the Third of France?" This selfish person is also very stupid, for nothing so augments conversation as a normal interest in other people.

> "I shook him well from side to side
>   Until his face was blue.
> Come, tell me how you live, I cried,
>   And what it is you do."

This plan of Alice's *Through the Looking Glass* ballad singer for shaking conversation out of people, tho somewhat too strenuous, is less fatiguing than Sherlock Holmes's inductive methods. Like Sherlock without his excuse, the kind and generous must confess to a colossal interest in the affairs of others. Gossip is the dialog of the drama of mankind; and we have a right to introduce any innocent and graceful means of thawing their stories from the actors, and of unraveling dramatic knots. People with keen judgment of men and things gather the harvest of a quiet eye; they see in the little world of private life histories as wonderful and issues as great as those that get our attention in literature, or in the theater, or in public life. Personal gossip in its intellectual form has a charm not unhealthy; and it gives new lights on character more often favorable than unfavorable.

There is no difference, between enjoying this personal talk and enjoying *The Mill on the Floss* or books of biography. Boswell, in his *Life of Johnson*, and Mrs. Thrale, in her *Letters*, were inveterate gossips about the great man. And what an incomparable little tattler was Fanny Burney—Madame d'Arblay! Lord William Lennox, in his *Drafts on My Memory*, is full of irrepressible and fascinating *memorabilia*, from the story of General Bullard's salad-dressing to important dramatic history connected with the theater of his time. The *Spectator* was the quintessence of gossip in an age of gossip and good conversation. We could go a great deal further back to the gossips of Theocritus, who are as living and life-like as if we had just met them in the park. All biography is a putting together of trifles which in the aggregate make up the engrossing life-stories of men and women of former and contemporary preeminence. It is to the gossips of all ages that we owe much of value in literary history.

Without the personal interest in the affairs of others which makes gossip possible, there would be no fellowship or warmth in life; social intercourse and conversation would be inhuman and lifeless. Mr. Benson in his essay "Conversation" tells us that an impersonal talker is likely to be a dull dog.

Mr. Henry van Dyke says that the quality of talkability does not mark a distinction among things; that it denotes a difference among people. And Chateaubriand, in his *Mémoirs d'Outre-tombe*, confides to us that he has heard some very pleasant reports become irksome and malicious in the mouths of ill-disposed verbal historians.

One can interest one's self in the dramatic incidents in the lives of one's acquaintances without ventilating or vilifying their character. Gossip is capable of a more genial purpose than traducing people. It is the malignity which turns gossip into scandal against which temperate conversationalists revolt; the sort of thing which Sheridan gibbeted in his celebrated play, *The School for Scandal*:

> "Give me the papers, (lisp)—how bold and free!
> Last night Lord L. was caught with Lady D.!
> . . . .
> "So strong, so swift, the monster there's no gagging:
> Cut scandal's head off, still the tongue is wagging."

But this is scandal, not gossip, and scandal comes from people incapable of anything better either in mind or conversation. Among those who understand the art of conversation, libelous talk is rarely heard; with those who cultivate it to perfection, never. It is the first commandment of the slanderer to repeat promptly all the vitriolic talk he hears, but to keep strictly to himself all pleasant words or kindly gossip. Those who draw no distinction between scandal and gossip should reflect that gossip may be good-natured and commendatory as well as hostile and adverse. In the published letters of the late James Russell Lowell is an account of his meeting Professor Mahaffy of Trinity College, Dublin, who is known to be one of the most agreeable of men. They met at the house of a friend in Birmingham, England, and when Lowell took leave of Mr. Mahaffy he said to his host: "Well, that's one of the most delightful fellows I ever met, and I don't mind if you tell him so!" When Lowell's remark was repeated to Mr. Mahaffy, he exclaimed, "Poor Lowell! to think that he can never have met an Irishman before!" And this was gossip as surely as the inimical prattle about Lord and Lady Byron was gossip. No, indeed, slander and libelous talk are not necessary ingredients of gossip. People who take malicious pleasure in using speech for malign purposes suffer from a mental disorder which does not come under the scope of conversation.

Regarding the mental deficiencies of those who love to wallow in the mire of salacious news about others, the psychologists have come to some interesting conclusions. To them it seems that there is an essential identity between the gossip and the genius. In both, the mental processes work with the same tendency to reproduce every fragment of past experience, because both think by what is known as "total recall." From the thought of one thing their minds pass to all sorts of remote connections, sane and silly, rational and grotesque, relevant and irrelevant. The essential difference between the gossip mind and the genius mind is the power of genius to distinguish between the worthy and the unworthy, the trivial and the relevant, the true and the false. The thoughts of the gossip, so the psychologists tell us, have connection but not coherence; the thoughts of the genius have coherence and likewise connection and unity. Thus we discover that scandal-mongers are at fault in the mind more than in the heart; and that it behooves people who do not wish to have themselves voted mentally defective to draw a distinction between scandal and innocent gossip. As I have already said, there is nothing so interesting as the dramatic incidents in the lives of human beings. Despite the nature-study enthusiasts who seem to refuse mankind a place in nature, "the proper study of mankind is man" and will forever remain so. But this does not mean that mental weaklings should be allowed to discover and talk about only salacious episodes in the history of their acquaintances. The vicious scandal-monger who defames another, or hears him defamed or scandalized, and then runs to him with enlarged and considerably colored tales of what was said about him, is the poison of the serpent and should not be tolerated in society. A sanitarium for mental delinquents is the only proper place for such a person.

And let me add that the apocryphal slanderer, the person who never says but hints all sorts of malicious things, is the worst sort of scandal-monger. The cultivated conversationalist who talks gossip in its intellectual form does not indulge in oblique hints and insinuations. He says what he has to say intrepidly because he says it discriminatingly.

Keen judgment which discovers the fundamental distinction between scandal and suitable personality in talk raises gossip to the perfection of an art and the dignity of a science. Undiscriminating people, therefore, had better leave personalities alone and stick to the more general and less resilient topics of conversation. Good gossip is attainable only by minds that are capable of much higher talk than gossip. Cultivated, well-poised, well-disposed persons need never be afraid of indulging their conversation to a certain extent with gossip, because they indulge it in the right way. And provided their personal and familiar talk is listened to by equally cultivated, well-poised, and well-disposed people, their gossip need not necessarily be limited to the mention of only pleasant and complimentary history; no more, indeed, than Plutarch found it necessary to tell of the glory of Demosthenes without mention that there were those who whispered graft and bribery in connection with his name. There are a few very good and very dull people who try to stop all adverse criticism. All raillery strikes them as cruel. They would like to see every parody murdered by the common hangman. Even the best of comedy is constitutionally repellent to them. They want only highly colored characters from which every mellow shade of fault has been obliterated. One cannot say that they have a real love of human nature, because they do not know what human nature is. They are ready to take up arms with it at every turn. Such people cannot see that ridicule, or gossip, can be either innocent or malignant; that history can be either prejudiced or unbiased.

With many, refusing to hear adverse criticism is a mere pose, while with others it is cynicism. In intercourse with the uneducated, any well-bred person is properly shocked by their pleasure in detraction and in bad news of all sorts. But the detestable people who seek every occasion to vilify, and who wish to hear only harm of the world, are so exceptional as to be negligible. These rare villains are eliminated when one speaks of inability to distinguish between detraction and adverse criticism. Those who can praise well are always adepts at criticizing adversely. They never carry their criticism too far, nor give purposely an acrid touch to it.

There is a grim tradition that a person should never say anything behind another's back which he would not say before his face. This is all very well so far as it relates to venomous tales repeated purposely to injure; but how colorless are the people who never have critical opinions on anything or anybody; or people who, having them, never express them! Criticism and cavil are two very different things. Absence of criticism is absence of the power of distinction. This age of science has taught people to look truth straight in the face and learn to discriminate. That person to whom everything is sweet does not know what sweet is. The sophisticated world, unlike the unsophisticated, is not afraid of "passing remarks." There is no doubt that criticism, whether it comes directly or roundabout, adds a terror to life as soon as one goes below a certain level of cultivation. The uneducated are frightened at the mere thought of criticism; the cultivated are not. Perhaps the reason for this difference is that ordinary people have a brutal and entirely uncritical criticism to fear. In that society sensitiveness is not very common. They are not dishonorable; they are merely hardy and can see no distinctions. It is not given to these people to praise rationally and to censure discriminatingly. Vilifying remarks are made and repeated among them which clever people would be incapable of uttering. The educated not only use a softened mode of speech, but they avoid repeating remarks, unless with a discerning wish to be helpful to others. The cultivated who have brought life to a far higher point than the uncultivated have protected their liberty by a social rule. They say what they like, and it does not get to the ears of the person about whom they have said it. And if it did it wouldn't much matter. Criticism which is critically given is usually critically received. The maliciousness of adverse criticism seldom lies in the person who voices it, but in the person who carries a tale. The moment sophisticated people learn that one among them has venomously repeated an adversely critical remark, they immediately know that that person is not to the manner born. There is no surer proof.

If the born advocate is not always a saint, the born critic is not always a sinner. Robert Louis Stevenson understood the importance of the personal touch in conversation when he wrote: "So far as conversational subjects are truly talkable, more than half of them may be reduced to three: that I am I, that you are you, and that there are other people dimly understood to be not quite the same as either." So, also, did Mr. J. M. Barrie, when he told us that his beloved Margaret Ogilvy, in spite of no personal interest in Gladstone, "had a profound faith in him as an aid to conversation. If there were silent men in the company, she would give him to them to talk about precisely as she would divide a cake among children."

It is often hinted by men that women are made good conversationalists by a sense of irresponsibility. But I am inclined to think that a little gossip now and then is relished by the best of men as well as women. The tendency to gossip with which men constantly credit women, and in which tendency the men themselves keep pace, helps both men and women very effectually to good conversation. "It is more important," says Stevenson again, "that a person should be a good gossip and talk pleasantly and smartly of common friends and the thousand and one nothings of the day and hour, than speak with the tongues of men and angels.... Talk is the creature of the street and market-place, feeding on gossip; and its last resort is still in a discussion on morals. That is the heroic form of gossip; heroic in virtue of its high pretensions; but still gossip because it turns on personalities."

Gossip, we must admit, has a perennial interest for all of us. Personal chat is the current coin of conversational capital. Society lives by gossip as it lives by bread. The most absurd rule in the world is to avoid personalities in conversation. To annihilate gossip would be to cut conversational topics in half. There is musical gossip, art gossip, theatrical gossip, literary gossip, and court gossip; there is political gossip, and fashionable gossip, and military gossip; there is mercantile gossip and commercial gossip of all kinds; there is physicians' gossip and professional gossip of every sort; there is scientists' gossip; and there is the gossip of the schools indulged in by masters and students all over the educational world. Of all the gossip in the world the most prodigious and prolific is religious gossip. Archbishops, bishops, deans, rectors, and curates are discussed unreservedly; and the questions put and answered are not whether they are apostolic teachers, but whether they are high, low, broad, or no church; whether they wear scarlet or black, intone or read, say "shibboleth" or "sibboleth."

The roots of gossip are deep in human interest; and, despite the nearly universal opinion of moralists, great reputations are more often built out of gossip than destroyed by it. Discriminating people do not create enemies by personalities, nor separate friends, because they gossip with a heart full of love, with charity for all, and with malice toward none. Gossip as a legitimate part of conversation is defended by one of the greatest of present-day scholars; and I cannot do better than to quote, in closing, what Mr. Mahaffy has said about it: "The topic which ought to be always interesting is the discussion of human character and human motives. If the novel be so popular a form of literature, how can the novel in real life fail to interest an intelligent company? People of serious temper and philosophic habit will be able to confine themselves to large ethical views and the general dealings of men; but to average people, both men and women, and perhaps most of all to busy men who desire to find in society relaxation from their toil, that lighter and more personal kind of criticism on human affairs will prevail which is known as gossip. It is idle to deny that there is no kind of conversation more fascinating than this. But its immorality may easily become such as to shock honest minds, and the man who indulges in it too freely at the expense of others will probably have to pay the cost of it himself in the long run; for those who hear him will fear him, and will retire into themselves in his presence. On the other hand, nothing is more honorable than to stand forth as the defender or the palliator of the faults imputed to others, and nothing is easier than to expand such a defense into general considerations as to the purity of human motives, which will raise the conversation from its unwholesome grounds into the upper air."

CHAPTER IV

WHAT SHOULD GUESTS TALK ABOUT AT DINNER?

"Good talk is not to be had for the asking. Humors must first be accorded in a kind of overture for prolog; hour, company, and circumstances be suited; and then at a fit juncture, the subject, the quarry of two heated minds, spring up like a deer out of the wood." Stevenson knew as well as Alice in Wonderland that something has to open the conversation. "You can't even drink a bottle of wine without opening it," argued Alice; and every dinner guest, during the quarter of an hour before dinner, has felt the sententiousness of her remark. Someone in writing about this critical period so conversationally difficult has contended that no person in his senses would think of wasting good talk in the drawing-room before dinner, but Professor Mahaffy thinks otherwise: "In the very forefront there stares us in the face that awkward period which even the gentle Menander notes as the worst possible for conversation, the short time during which people are assembling, and waiting for the announcement of dinner. If the witty man were not usually a selfish person, who will not exhibit his talent without the reward of full and leisurely appreciation, this is the real moment to show his powers. A brilliant thing said at the very start which sets people laughing, and makes them forget that they are waiting, may alter the whole complexion of the party, may make the silent and distant people feel themselves drawn into the sympathy of common merriment, and thaw the iciness which so often fetters Anglo-Saxon society. But as this faculty is not given to many, so the average man may content himself with having something ready to tell, and this, if possible, in answer to the usual question exprest or implied: Is there any news this afternoon? There are few days that the daily paper will not afford to the intelligent critic something ridiculous either in style or matter which has escaped the ordinary public; some local event, nay, even some local tragedy, may suggest a topic not worth more than a few moments of attention, which will secure the interest of minds vacant, and perhaps more hungry to be fed than their bodies. Here then, if anywhere in the whole range of conversation, the man or woman who desires to be agreeable may venture to think beforehand, and bring with them something ready, merely as the first kick or starting point to make the evening run smoothly." However this may be, it is only with that communicative feeling which comes after eating and drinking that talkers warm up to discriminating discussion; and in the drawing-room just before dinner, one can scarcely expect the conversation to turn on anything but trifles.

At the moment a man presents his arm to the woman he is to take in to dinner, he must have something ready in the way of a remark, for if he goes in in silence, he is lost. There are a thousand and one nothings he may say at this time. I know a clever man who talks interestingly for fifteen minutes about the old-fashioned practice of offering a woman the hand to lead her in to dinner, and whether or not that custom was more courteous and graceful than our modern way of proceeding.

The question is often asked, "What should guests talk about at a dinner?" I restrict my interrogation to guests, because there is a distinction between the directing of a dinner-guest's conversation and the guiding of the talk by host or hostess into necessary or interesting channels. Dinners, especially in diplomatic circles, are as often given to bring about dexterously certain ends in view as they are given for mere pleasure; and when this is the case it is necessary as well as gracious to steer conversation along the paths that it should go. A guest's first duty is to his dinner-companion, the person with whom, according to the prearranged plan of the hostess, he enters the dining-room and by whom he finds himself seated at table. His next duty is to his hosts. He has also an abstract conversational duty to his next nearest neighbor at table. It is every guest's duty, too, to keep his ears open and be ready to join in general talk should the host or hostess attempt to draw all their guests into any general discussion.

The best answer to the question, "What should guests at dinner talk about?" is, anything and everything, provided the talk is tinctured with tact, discretion, and discrimination. To one's dinner-companion, if he happens to be a familiar acquaintance, one can even forget to taboo dress, disease, and domestics. One might likewise, with discretion, set at liberty the usually forbidden talk of "shop," on condition that such intimate conversation is to one's dinner-companion alone and is not dragged into the general flights of the table-talk. While one talks to one's dinner-companion in a low voice, however, it needs nice discrimination not to seem to talk under one's breath, or to say anything to a left-hand neighbor which would not be appropriate for a right-hand neighbor to hear. When in general talk, the habit some supposedly well-bred persons have of glancing furtively at any one guest to interrogate telepathically another's opinion of some remark is bad taste beyond the power of censure or the possibility of forgiveness.

At large, formal dinners, on the order of banquets, it would be impossible for all guests to include a host or hostess in their conversational groups from any and every part of the table; only those guests seated near them can do this. But at small, informal dinners all guests should, whenever possible, consider it their duty to direct much of their conversation to their host and hostess. I have seen guests at small dinners of no more than six or eight covers go through the various courses of a three hours' dining, ignoring their host and hostess in the entire table-talk, while conversing volubly with others. There is something more due a host and hostess than mere greetings on entering and leave-takings on departing. If the dinner-party is so large that all guests cannot show them at the table the attention due them, the delinquent ones can at least seek an opportunity in the drawing-room, after guests have left the dining-room, to pay their host and hostess the proper courtesy. Hosts should never be made to feel that it is to their cook they owe their distinction, and to their table alone that guests pay visits.

To say that the dominant note in table-talk should be light and humorous is going too far; but conversation between dinner-companions should tend strongly to the humorous, to the light, to the small change of ideas. There should be an adroit intermixing of light and serious talk. I noted once with keen interest a shrewd mingling of serious talk and small talk at a dinner given to a distinguished German scientist.

A clever woman of my acquaintance found herself the one selected to entertain at table this foreigner and scholar. When she was presented in the drawing-room to the eminent man who was to take her in to dinner, her hostess opened the conversation by informing the noted guest that his new acquaintance, just that morning, had had conferred upon her the degree of doctor of philosophy, which was the reason she had been assigned as dinner-companion to so profound a man. The foreigner followed the conversational cue, recounting to his companion his observations on the number of American women seeking higher education, *et cetera*. Such a conversational situation was little conducive to small talk; but on the way from the drawing-room to the dining-table, this clever woman directed the talk into light vein by assuring the scholar and diplomat that there was nothing dangerous about her even if she did possess a university degree; that she would neither bite nor philosophize on all occasions; that she was quite as full of life and frolic as if she had never seen a university. You can imagine the effect of this vivacity upon the profoundest of men, and you can see how this clever woman's ability at small talk made a comrade of a notable academician. As the dinner progressed the talk between these two wavered from jest to earnest in a most charming manner. Apropos of a late book on some serious subject not expurgated for babes and sucklings, but written for thinking men and women, the German scientist asked if he might present his companion with a copy, provided he promised to glue carefully together the pages unfit for frolicking feminine minds. Two days later she received the book with some of the margins pasted—which pages, of course, were the first ones she read.

When making an attempt to sparkle in small talk, dinner-guests should remember that the line of demarcation between light talk and buffoonery may become dangerously delicate. One can talk lightly, but nicely; while buffoonery is just what the lexicographers define it to be: "Amusing others by clownish tricks and by commonplace pleasantries." Gentle dulness ever loved a joke; and the fact that very often humorists, paid so highly in literature to perform, will not play a single conversational trick, is the best proof that they have the good sense to vote their hosts and companions capable of being entertained by something nobler than mere pleasantry. "When wit," says Sydney Smith, "is combined with sense and information; when it is in the hands of one who can use it and not abuse it (and one who can despise it); who can be witty and something more than witty; who loves decency and good nature ten thousand times better than wit,—wit is then a beautiful and delightful part of conversation."

Opinions as to what good nature is would perhaps vary. "You may be good-natured, sir," said Boswell to Doctor Johnson, "but you are not good-humored." The speech of men and women is diverse and variously characteristic. All people say "good morning," but no two of God's creatures say it alike. Their words range from a grunt to gushing exuberance; and one is as objectionable as the other. Even weighty subjects can be talked about in tones of badinage and good breeding. Plato in his wonderful conversations always gave his subject a fringe of graceful wit, but beneath the delicate shell there was invariably a hard nut to be cracked. If good nature above all is sincere, it will escape being gushing. The hypocrisy which says, "My dear Mrs. So-and-so, I'm perfectly delighted to see you; do sit right down on this bent pin!" is not good nature; it is pure balderdash.

Thoughtful dinner-guests take pains not to monopolize the conversation. They bring others of the company into their talk, giving them opportunities of talking in their turn, and listening themselves while they do so: "You, Mr. Brown, will agree with me in this"; or, "Mr. Black, you have had more experience in such cases than I have; what is your opinion?" The perfection of this quality of conversational charm consists in that rare gift, the art of drawing others out, and is as valuable and graceful in guests as in hosts.

The French have some dinner-table conventions which to us seem strange. At any small dining of eight or ten people the talk is always supposed to be general. The person who would try to begin a *tête-à-tête* conversation with the guest sitting next to him at table would soon find out his mistake. General conversation is as much a part of the repast as the viands; and wo to the unwary mortals who, tempted by short distances, start to chatter among themselves. A diner-out must be able to hold his own in a conversation in which all sorts of distant, as well as near, contributors take part. Of course, this implies small dinners; but English-speaking people, even in small gatherings, do not attempt general conversation to such an extent. They consider it a difficult matter to accomplish the diagonal feat of addressing guests at too great a distance.

Dinner-companions, however, should be alert to others of the conversational group. A guest can as easily lead the talk into general paths as can a host or hostess. Indeed, it is gracious for him to do this, tho it is not his duty. The duty lies entirely with a host or hostess. At any time through the dinner a guest can help to make conversation general: If some one has just told in a low voice, to a right-hand or left-hand neighbor alone, some clever impersonal thing, or a good anecdote, or some interesting happening suitable to general table-talk, the guest can get the attention of all present by addressing some one at the furthest point of the table from him: "Mr. Snow, Miss Frost has just told me something which will interest you, I know, and perhaps all of us: Miss Frost, please tell Mr. Snow about," *et cetera*. Miss Frost, then, speaking a little louder in order that Mr. Snow may hear, engages the attention of the entire table. The moment any one round the table thus invites the attention of the whole dinner-group, dinner-companions should drop instantly their private chats and join in whatever general talk may ensue on the topic generally introduced. The thread of their *tête-à-tête* conversation can be taken up later as the general table-talk is suspended.

A narration or an anecdote should not be long drawn out. A dinner-guest, or a host, or a hostess, is for the time being a conversationalist, not a lecturer. It is the unwritten law of successful dinner-talk that no one person round the table should keep the floor for more than a few short sentences. The point in anecdotes should be brought out quickly, and no happening of long duration should be recounted. A guest in telling any experience can break his own narration up into conversation by drawing into his talk, or recital, others who are interested in his hobby or in his experience. Responses to toasts at banquets may be somewhat longer than the individual speeches of a single person in general table-talk; but any dinner-speaker knows that even his response runs the risk of being spoiled if extended beyond a few minutes.

There are never-failing topics of interest and untold material out of which to weave suitable dinner-talk, provided it is woven in the right way. And this weaving of talk is an art in which one may become proficient by giving it attention, just as one becomes the master of any other art by taking thought and probing into underlying principles. So in the art of talking well, even naturally fluent talkers need by faithful pains to get beyond the point where they only happen to talk. They need to attain that conscious power over conversational situations which gives them precision and grace in adapting means to ends and a fine discrimination in choosing among their resources.

A one-sided conversation between companions is deadly unless discrimination is used in the matter of listening as well as talking. For instance:

Mr. Cook: "Don't you think the plan of building a great riverside drive a splendid one?"

Miss Brown: "Yes."

Mr. Cook: "The New York drive is one of the joys of life; it gives more unalloyed pleasure than anything I know of."

Miss Brown: "Yes."

Unless under conditions suitable to listening and not to talking, Mr. Cook might feel like saying to Miss Brown, as a bright young man once said to a quiet, beautiful girl: "For heaven's sake, Miss Mary, say something, even if you have to take it back." While it is true that listening attentively is as valuable and necessary to thoroughly good conversation as is talking one's self, good listening demands the same discretion and discrimination that good talking requires. It is the business of any supposedly good conversationalist to discern when and why one must give one's companion over to soliloquy, and when and why one must not do so.

The dining-room is both an arena in which talkers fight with words upon a field of white damask, and a love-feast of discussion. If guests are neither hatefully disputatious, nor hypocritically humble, if they are generous, frank, natural, and wholly honest in word and mind, the impression they make cannot help being agreeable.

CHAPTER V

THE TALK OF HOST AND HOSTESS AT DINNER

Sydney Smith, by all accounts a great master of the social art, said of himself: "There is one talent I think I have to a remarkable degree: there are substances in nature called amalgams, whose property it is to combine incongruous materials. Now I am a moral amalgam, and have a peculiar talent for mixing up human materials in society, however repellent their natures." "And certainly," adds his biographer, "I have seen a party composed of materials as ill-sorted as could possibly be imagined, drawn out and attracted together, till at last you would believe they had been born for each other."

But this rôle of moral amalgam is such a difficult one, it must be performed with such tact and delicacy, that hostesses are justified in employing whatever mechanical aids are at their command. In dinner-giving, the first process of amalgamation is to select congenial people. Dinners are very often flat failures conversationally because guests are invited at random. Choosing the lesser of two evils, it is better to run the risk of offending than to jeopardize the flow of talk by inviting uncongenial people. When dinners are given to return obligations it is not always easy to arrange profitably the inviting and seating of guests. But the judgment displayed just here makes or mars a dinner. A good way out of the difficulty, where hosts have obligations to people of different tastes and interests, is to give a series of dinners, and to send the invitations out at the same time. If Mrs. X. is asked to dine with Mrs. Z. the evening following the dinner to which Mrs. Z. has invited Mrs. Y., Mrs. X. is not offended.

To see that there is no failure of tact in seating guests should be the next process of amalgamation. To get the best results a great deal of care should be bestowed upon the mixture of this human salad. Guests should be seated in such a way that neighbors at table will interest each other; a brilliant guest should be placed where he may at least snatch crumbs of intellectual comfort if his near companions, tho talkative, are not conversationalists of the highest order; the loquacious guest should be put next to the usually taciturn, provided he is one who can be roused to conversation when thrown with talkable people. Otherwise one of the hosts should devote himself to the business of promoting talk with the uncommunicative but no less interesting person. A wise hostess will consider this matter of seating guests in connection with selecting and inviting them. It is, therefore, one of the subordinate and purely mechanical processes of the real art of amalgamation.

If hosts forget nothing that will tempt a guest to his comfort, they will remember above all the quarter of an hour before dinner, and will begin the actual conquest of amalgamation while their friends are assembling. By animation and cordiality they will put congenial guests in conversation with each other, and will bring forth their mines of things old and new, coining the ore into various sums, large and small, as may be needed.

In some highly cultured circles, men and women are supposed to be sufficiently educated and entertaining to require no literary or childish aids to conversation. Every dinner-giver, however, knows the device of suitable quotations, or original sayings, or clever limericks, on place-cards, and the impetus they give to conversation between dinner-companions as the guests are seated. But the responsibility of host and hostess does not end when they thus furnish dinner-companions a conversational cue. "This is why," as has been well said by Canon Ainger, "a dinner party to be good for anything, beyond the mere enjoyment of the menu, should be neither too large nor too small. Some forgotten genius laid it down that the number should never be less than that of the Graces, nor more than that of the Muses, and the latter half of the epigram may be safely accepted. Ten as a maximum, eight for perfection; for then conversation can be either dialog, or may spread and become general, and the host or hostess has to direct no more than can profitably be watched over. It is the dinner party of sixteen to twenty that is so terrible a risk.... Good general conversation at table among a few is now rather the exception, from the common habit of crowding our rooms or our tables and getting rid of social obligations as if they were commercial debts. Indeed many of our young people have so seldom heard a general conversation that they grow up in the belief that their only duty in society will be to talk to one man or woman at a time. So serious are the results of the fashion of large dinner parties. For really good society no dinner-table should be too large to exclude general conversation." At a banquet of thirty or forty, for instance, general talk is impossible. At such banquets toasts and responses take the place of general talk; but at small dinners it is gracious for a host and hostess to lead the conversation often into general paths. Ignoring a host and hostess through the various courses of a three hours' dining, which I have already mentioned, can as easily be the fault of the host and hostess themselves as it can be due to inattention on the part of guests. A host and hostess should no more ignore any one guest than any one guest should ignore them; and if they sit at their own table, as I have sometimes seen hosts and hostesses do, assuming no different function in the conversation than if they were the most thoughtless guest at the table of another, they cannot expect their own guests to be anything but petrified, however instinctively social.

The conversational duty of a host and hostess is, therefore, to the entire company of people assembled at their board, as well as especially to their right-hand neighbors, the guests of honor. It is the express function of a host and hostess to see that each guest takes active part in general table-talk. Leading the talk into general paths and drawing guests out thus become identical. It is this promoting of general conversation which is the backbone of all good talk. Many people, however, do not need to be drawn out. Mr. Mahaffy cautions: "Above all, the particular guest of the occasion, or the person best known as a wit or story-teller, should not be pressed or challenged at the outset, as if he were manifestly exploited by the company." Such a guest can safely be left quite to himself, unless he is a stranger. As drawing out the people by whom one finds one's self surrounded in society will be treated in a forthcoming essay, I shall not deal with it here further than to tell how a famous pun of Charles Lamb's gave a thoughtful host not only the means of swaying the conversation of the entire table to a subject of universal interest, but as well the means of drawing out a well-informed yet timid girl. Guiding his talk with his near neighbor into a discussion of the *pros* and *cons* of punning, he attracted the attention of all his guests by addressing some one at the further end of the table: "Mr. White, we were speaking of punning as a form of wit, and it reminded me that I have heard Miss Black, at your left, repeat a clever pun of Charles Lamb's—a retort he made when some one accused him of punning. Miss Black, can you give us that pun? I'm afraid I've forgotten it." In order that her host and all the table might hear her distinctly, Miss Black pitched her voice a little higher than in talk with her near neighbors and responded quickly: "I'll try to remember it, yes:

> "'If I were punish-ed
> For every pun I've shed,
> I should not have a puny shed
>   Wherein to lay my punished head!'"

Thus Miss Black was not only drawn out, she was also drawn *into* the conversation and became the center of an extended general discussion on the very impersonal and interesting subject of punning. As the talk on punning diverged, the conversation gradually fell back into private chats between dinner-companions.

A host or hostess will know intuitively when the conversation has remained *tête-à-tête* long enough, and will once more make it general. When guests pay due attention to their host and hostess, the talk will naturally be carried into general channels, especially where guests are seated a little distance away. Even in general conversation a good story, if short and crisp, is no doubt a good thing; but when either a host or a guest does nothing but "anecdote" from the soup to the coffee, story-telling becomes tiresome. Anecdotes should not be dragged in by the neck, but should come naturally as the talk about many different subjects may suggest them.

It is the duty of the host and hostess, and certainly their pleasure, to make conversational paths easy for any strangers in a strange land. It does not follow that a host and hostess are always well acquainted with all their guests. There are instances where they have never even met some of them. An invitation is extended to the house-guest of a friend; or some person of distinction temporarily in the vicinity is invited, the formality of previous calls being waived for this reason or that. Unless a hostess can feel perfectly safe in delegating to some one else the entertaining of a stranger, it is wise to seat this guest as near to herself as possible, even tho he is not made a guest of honor. She can thus learn something about her new acquaintance and put the stranger on an equal conversational footing with the guests who know each other well.

In their zeal to give their friends pleasure, a host or hostess often tells a guest that he is to take a particularly brilliant woman in to dinner, and the woman is informed that she is to be the neighbor of a notably clever man. To one whose powers are brought out by being put on his mettle this might prove the best sort of conversational tonic; on the other hand it might be better tact to say that tho a certain person has the reputation of being exceptionally clever, he is, in truth, as natural as an old shoe; that all one has to do to entertain him is to talk ordinarily about commonplace topics. In ninety-nine cases out of a hundred this is so. Some one is responsible for the epigram: "A great man always lives a great way off"; and it is true that when we come to know really great people we find that they are as much interested as any one else in the commonplaces of life. Indeed, the more intellectual people are, the more the homely things of life interest them. When Tennyson was once a passenger on a steamer crossing the English Channel, some people who had been assigned to seats opposite him in the dining saloon learned that their neighbor at table was the great poet. In a flutter of interest they listened for the wisdom which would drop from the distinguished man's mouth and heard the hearty words, "What fine potatoes these are!" This particular point requires nice discernment on the part of host and hostess; they should know when they may safely impress one guest with the cleverness of the other, and when it would be disastrous to do so. Suppose the consequence is that each guest waits for the sparkling flow of wit from the other, and to the consternation of the host and hostess there is profound silence between two really interesting people on whose cleverness they had counted to make their dinner a success!

It is also the province of a host and hostess tactfully to steer the drift of general table-talk away from topics likely to offend the sensibilities of any one guest. Hosts owe not only attention but protection to every person whom they ask to their home, and it devolves upon them to interpose and come to the rescue if a guest is disabled in any way from doing himself any sort of conversational justice. Swaying conversation round and over topics embarrassing to any guest requires the utmost tact and delicacy on the part of a host and hostess; for in keeping one guest from being wounded or embarrassed, the offender himself must not be made to feel conscious of his misstep. Indeed he may be, and usually is, quite unconscious of the effect his words are having on those whom he does not know well. Any subject which is being handled dangerously must be *juggled* out of sight, and the determination to juggle it must be concealed. Tho it is quite correct for one to say one's self, "I beg pardon for changing the subject abruptly," nothing is worse form than to say to another, "Change the subject," or, "Let us change the subject." To do this is both rude and crude. Directing conversation means leading talkers unconsciously to talk of something else. Any guest, as well as a host or hostess, may graciously steer conversation when it touches a subject some phase of which is likely to offend sensitive and unsophisticated people. At a series of dinners given to a circle of philosophic minds religious intolerance was largely the subject of discussion. The circle, for the most part well known to each other, was of liberal belief. A guest appeared among them, and it was known only to one or two that this man was a sincere Catholic. As the talk turned upon religious discussion, one of the guests so directed the conversation as to bring out the information that the stranger was a Catholic by faith and rearing. This was a very kind and appropriate thing to do. It acquainted the hostess with a fact of which she was ignorant; and it gave all present a feeling of security in whatever they might say.

A hospitable host and hostess will not absorb the conversation at their table. They will render the gracious service of furnishing a background for the cleverness of others, rather than display unsparingly their own brilliancy. Indeed, a man or woman does not have to be brilliant or intellectual to succeed in this most gracious of social arts. The host or hostess who possesses sympathy and tact will surpass in dinner-giving the most brilliant person in the world who selfishly monopolizes conversation at his own table. If guests cannot go away from a dinner-table feeling better pleased with themselves, that campaign of hospitality has been a failure. When the self-satisfaction on their faces betrays the subtle art of the host and hostess in having convinced all their guests that they have made themselves interesting, then the acme of hospitality has been achieved. One of the most good-natured but most inane of men was one day chuckling at having been royally diverted at a dinner-party.

"He was at Mrs. X's," said some one.

"How do you know that?"

"Indeed! Don't I know her way? She'd make a raven go home rivaling the nightingale."

To be able to make your guests better pleased with themselves is the greatest of all social accomplishments.

"An ideal dinner party," says a famous London hostess, "resembles nothing so much as a masterpiece of the jeweler's art in the center of which is some crystalline gem in the form of a sparkling and sympathetic hostess round whom the guests are arranged in an effective setting." It would seem quite as necessary that a host prove a crystalline gem in this masterpiece of the jeweler's art. To be signally successful at dinner-giving, care to make the talk interesting is as necessary as care in the preparation of viands. Really successful hosts and hostesses take as much precaution against fatalities in conversation as against those which offend the palate. While attending carefully to the polishing of the crystal and to the preparing of the menu which will make their table a delight, they remember that the intellect of their guests must be satisfied no less than their eyes and their stomachs.

CHAPTER VI

INTERRUPTION IN CONVERSATION

Interruption, more surely than anything else, kills conversation. The effusive talker who, in spite of his facility for words, is in no sense a conversationalist, refuses to recognize the fact that conversation involves a partnership; that in this company of joint interest each party has a right to his turn in the conversational engagement. He ignores his conversational partners; he breaks into their sentences with his own speech before they have their words well out of their mouths. He has grown so habitual in his interrupting that he rattles on unconscious of the disgust he is producing in the mind of any well-bred, discriminating conversationalist who hears him. The best of talkers interrupt occasionally in conversation; but the unconscious, rude interruption of the habitual interrupter, and the unintentional, conscious interruption of the cultivated talker are easily discernible, and are two very different things.

We are accustomed to think that children are the only offenders in interrupting; but, shades of the French *salon*, the crimes of the adults! The great pity about this positive phase of interrupting is that all habitual interrupters are totally unconscious that they continually break into the speeches of their conversers and literally knock their very words back into their mouths. Robert Louis Stevenson pronounced this eulogy over his friend, James Walter Ferrier: "He was the only man I ever knew who did not habitually interrupt." Now, you who read this may not believe that you are one of the violators of this first commandment of good conversation, "thou shalt not interrupt"; but stop to think what small chance you have of escape when only *one* acquaintance of Stevenson's was acquitted of this crime. One must become conscious of the fact that he continually interrupts before he can cease interrupting. The unconsciousness is what constitutes the crime; for conscious interruption ceases to be interruption. The moment a good talker is aware of having broken into the speech of his converser, he forestalls interruption by waiting to hear what was about to be said. He instantly cuts off his own speech with the conventional courtesy-phrase, "I beg your pardon," which is the same as saying, "Pardon me for seeming to be unwilling to listen to you; I really am both willing and glad to hear what you have to say." And he proves his willingness by waiting until the other person can finish the thought he ventured upon. What better proof that conversation is listening as well as talking?

Sheer, nervous inability to listen is responsible for one phase of interruption to conversation. It is the interruption of the wandering eye which tells that one's words have not been heard. "The person next to you must be bored by my conversation, for it is going into one of your ears and out of the other," said a talker rather testily to his inattentive dinner-companion whose absent-minded and tardy replies had been snapping the thread of the thought until it grew intolerable. She was perhaps only a little less irritating than the man who became so unconscious in the habit of inattention that on one occasion his converser had scarcely finished when he began abstractedly: "Yes, very odd, very odd," and told the identical anecdote all over again.

There is another phase of interrupting which proceeds from the jerky talker whose remarks are not provoked by what his conversational partner is saying, with observation and answer, affirmation and rejoinder, but who waits breathlessly for a pause to jump in and tell some thought of his own. Of this sort of talker Dean Swift wrote: "There are people whose manners will not suffer them to interrupt you directly, but what is almost as bad, will discover abundance of impatience, and lie upon the watch until you have done, because they have started something in their own thoughts, which they long to be delivered of. Meantime, they are so far from regarding what passes that their imaginations are wholly turned upon what they have in reserve, for fear it should slip out of their memory; and thus they confine their invention, which might otherwise range over a hundred things full as good, and that might be much more naturally introduced." An anecdote or a remark will keep. We are not under the necessity of begrudging every moment that shortens our own innings; of interrupting our companion by our looks and voting him an impediment to our own much better remarks.

A less objectionable phase of interrupting, because it as often springs from kind thought as from arrogance, is that of the conversationalist so anxious to prove his quickness of perception that he assumes to know what you are going to say before you have finished your sentence in your own mind, and to put an interpretation on your arguments before you are done stating them. His interpretation is as often exactly the opposite of your own as it is identical; and, right or wrong, the foisted-in explanation serves only to interrupt the sequence of thought. As early as 1832 a writer in the *New England Magazine* waxed wroth to pugilistic outburst against this form of interruption: "I have heard individuals praised for this, as indicating a rapidity of mind which arrived at the end before the other was half through. But I should feel as much disposed to knock a man down who took my words out of my mouth, as one who stole my money out of my pocket. Such a habit may be a credit to one's powers, but not to one's modesty or good feeling. What is it but saying, 'My dear sir, you are making a very bungling piece of work with that sentence of yours; allow me to finish it for you in proper style.'" Tho one is inclined to feel that this author could well have reserved his verbal scourging for more irritating forms of impertinent interruption, it is nevertheless true that people are more entirely considerate who allow their conversational partners to finish their statements without fear of being tript up.

It is only lack of discrimination on the part of glib talkers to suppose that those who express themselves more deliberately are less interesting in conversation. The pig is one of the most rapidly loquacious of animals, yet no one would say that the pig is an attractive conversationalist. Pope may have been slow in forming the mosaic of symbols which express so superbly the fact that

> "Words are like leaves; and where they most abound
> Much fruit of sense beneath is rarely found,"

but his deliberateness did not dim the wisdom, or interest, or beauty, of his lines. Slow talkers, if allowed to express themselves in their own way, only add to the attractiveness of any group. Why should we enjoy characterization more in literature and in drama than in life? "Good talking," says Stevenson, "is declarative of the man; it is dramatic like an impromptu piece of acting where each should represent himself to the greatest advantage; and that is the best kind of talk where each speaker is most fully and candidly himself, and where, if you should shift the speeches round from one to another, there would be the greatest loss in significance and perspicuity."

The Gradgrinds of society who are always coming down upon us with some horrible and unnecessary piece of fact are another form of interruption to good conversation. They stop you to remind you that the accident happened in Tremont Street, not in Boylston; and they suspend a pertinent point in the air to inform you that it was Mr. Jones's eldest sister, not his youngest, who was abroad at the time of the San Francisco earthquake. If some one refers to an incident as having occurred on the tenth of the month, they deem it necessary to stop the talker because they happen to know that it was on the ninth. People are often their own Gradgrinds, interrupting themselves in the midst of a narration to correct some trivial mistake which has no bearing one way or the other on what they are saying.

Many otherwise good talkers are at times afflicted with aphasia and lose the simplest and most familiar word at just the crucial moment—the very word which is necessary to the point they wish to make. This happens more often with elderly people; and it was on such an occasion that I heard a catchword fiend, a moderately young person, use her pet phrase as a red lantern to stop better, if more halting, talk. "Mr. Black was telling me to-day about Mr. White's being appointed to —— what do you call that office?" implored the dignified matron. "Just call it anything, Mrs. Gray, a bandersnatch, or a buttonhook, or a battering-ram," impertinently suggested the glib undergraduate who had been applying these words to everybody and everything, and who continued to do so until she had found a new catchword as the main substance of her conversation. The infirmities of age, as well as the mellowed wisdom of it, deserve the utmost consideration, especially from youth; and in this instance deference in aiding the elderly woman to find her word would have been more graceful than pleasantry, even if the pleasantry were of a less spurious kind.

Conversation suffers from outside interruptions as much as from interrupting directly within the conversational group. Bringing very little children into grown-up company led Charles Lamb to propose the health of Herod, King of the Jews! Society is no place for young children; and if older children are permitted to be present they should be led to listen attentively and to join the conversation modestly. If a child ventures an opinion or asks a question concerning the topic he is hearing discust, he should be welcomed into the conversation. His views should, in this case, be given the same consideration, no matter how immature, as the riper views of his elders; he should be made a legitimate part of the conversational group. Either this, or he should be sent entirely away. There are no half measures in a matter of this sort. The parent's reiterated commands to "keep quiet," or "to be seen and not heard," interrupt as much as the child's prattle. Furthermore, many a child's natural aptitude for talking well has been crusht by older people stifling every thought the youngster attempted to utter. A bright young girl of my acquaintance was so supprest by her parents from the age of seven to fifteen that she early acquired the habit of never opening her mouth without first getting the consent of father's eyebrow, or mother's. A child thus treated in youth grows up to be timid and halting in speech; his individuality and spontaneity are smothered. Either let the children talk, meanwhile teaching them *how* to converse, or send them off to themselves where they may at least express their thoughts to citizens of their own age. The very best conversational lesson that a child can be given is imparted when he is taught not to interrupt; when he is made to understand that he must either talk according to the niceties of thoroughly good conversation or must be sent away.

It is often contended that children are out of place at a dining-table where even tolerable conversation is supposed to be carried on. This view is no doubt well taken regarding formal dinners; but round the family board is the best place in the world to implant in children the principles of good conversation and interesting table-talk. To this end family differences and unpleasantnesses should be left behind when the family goes to the table. Parents should insist, as far as possible, that their children discuss at the dining-table only the pleasant and interesting happenings of the day. "First of all," says Mr. Mahaffy, "let me warn those who think it is not worth while taking trouble to talk in their family circle, or who read the newspaper at meals, that they are making a mistake which has far-reaching consequences. It is nearly as bad as those convent schools or ladies' academies, where either silence or a foreign tongue is imposed at meals. Whatever people may think of the value of theory, there is no doubt whatever that practise is necessary for conversation; and it is at home among those who are intimate, and free in expressing their thoughts, that this practise must be sought. It is thus, and thus only, that young people can go out into the world properly provided with the only universal introduction to society—agreeable speech and manner."

Trampling on the social and conversational rights of the young was some time ago so well commented upon in *The Outlook* that I transfer part of the article to these pages. The editorial emphasized also the educational advantages of good table-talk in the home: "There is no educational opportunity in the home more important than the talk at table. Children who have grown up in homes in which the talk ran on large lines and touched all the great interests of life will agree that nothing gave them greater pleasure or more genuine education.... Perhaps one reason why some American children are aggressive and lacking in respect is the frivolity of the talk that goes on in some American families. If children are in the right atmosphere they will not be intrusive or impertinent. Make place for their interests, their questions, the problems of their experience; for there are young as well as old perplexities. Encourage them to talk, and meet them more than half-way by the utmost hospitality to the subjects that interest and puzzle them. Give them serious attention; do not ridicule their confusion of statement nor belittle their troubles.... Do not limit the talk at table to the topics of childhood, but make it intelligible to children. Some people make the mistake of 'talking down' to their children; of turning the conversation at table into a kind of elaborate 'baby-talk'; not realizing that they are robbing their children of hearing older people talk about the world in which they live. The child is always looking ahead, peering curiously into the mysterious world round him, hearing strange voices from it, getting wonderful glimpses into it. At night when the murmur of voices comes upstairs, he hears in it the sounds of a future full of great things.... It is not, therefore, the child of six who sits at the table and listens; it is a human spirit, eager, curious, wondering, surrounded by mysteries, silently taking in what it does not understand to-day, but which will take possession of it next year and become a torch to light it on its way. It is through association with older people that these fructifying ideas come to the child; it is through such talk that he finds the world he is to possess.... The talk of the family ought not, therefore, to be directed at him or shaped for him; but it ought never to forget him; it ought to make a place for him."

Apropos of children's appreciation of good talk, this story is told of a young son of one of the clever men of Chicago: Guests were present and the boy sat quietly listening to the brilliant conversation of his elders, when his father suggested to Paul that it was late and perhaps he had better go to bed.

"Please, father, let me stay," pleaded the youngster, "I do so enjoy interesting conversation." Another and as deep a childlike appreciation comes from the classic city of our American Cambridge. The little daughter of one of its representative families had lain awake for hours upstairs straining her ears to hear the conversation from below. When her mother came into the little one's room after her guests had gone, the tiny lady said plaintively, "Mother dear, while I've been lying here all alone you were having such a liberal time downstairs." Unconscious recognition of his just right to converse occasionally with older people was exprest naïvely by the little son of a prominent Atlanta family when visiting friends on a plantation. "I like to stay here because you let me talk every day at the table," answered John, when his host asked him why he was pleased in the country. "Don't they let you talk every day at home, John?" "Oh, when father says 'give the kiddo a chance,' then they let me talk." This appreciation of his host's welcoming him into the conversation was a rare compliment from little John to his older friends and to their interest in child-life.

Another external and demoralizing interruption to talk is poor table-service. There can be no good conversation at table where the talk is constantly interrupted by wordy instructions to servants. A hostess who takes pride in the table-talk of her guests assures herself in advance that the maid or the butler serving the table is well trained, in order that no questions of servants can jeopardize the flow of conversation. If anything makes it necessary for serving maid or butler to confer with host or hostess, it should be done in an undertone so that conversation is not interrupted. But no matter how quietly the servant does this, the conversation *is* interrupted by the mere fact that the attention of the host or hostess is diverted for even a moment from the subject being discust. In the home, as in the business office, efficient help means efficient management. It is a reflection on any hostess to have her table served so badly three hundred and sixty-five days in the year that the service is an interruption to table-talk. If she were capable herself, she would have a capable, well-trained maid or butler. If a maid or butler could not be trained properly, her capability would show itself in dismissing that servant and getting one who could be trained. To the end that conversation will not be interrupted, the "Russian" method of dining-table service is preferable to all others, and is becoming as popular in America as in the rest of the world.[A]

A host and hostess can themselves, by the very atmosphere they create, become an unconscious element of interruption to table-talk. To insure fluent conversation at table, hosts must be free from worry; they must cultivate imperturbability; they must be able to ignore or smile at any accident which might happen "in the best regulated family." There is nothing more distasteful to guests than to observe that their host is anxious lest the arrangements of the hostess miscarry, or that their hostess is making herself quite wretched by a fear that the dishes will not be prepared to perfection, or over the breaking of some choice bit of crystal. At a dinner recently I saw the hostess nervous enough to weep over an accident which demolished a treasured salad bowl; and the result was that it took strong effort on the part of a self-sacrificing and friendly guest to keep up the pleasant flow of talk. How much more tactful and delightful was the manner in which another hostess treated a similar situation. The guests were startled by a crash in the butler's pantry, and every one knew from the tinkling sound that it was cut glass. After a few words of instruction quietly given, the hostess laughingly said, "I hope there is enough glass in reserve so that none of you dear people will have to drink champagne from teacups." This was not only a charming, informal way of smoothing out an awkward situation, but it gave the poor butler the necessary confidence to finish serving the dinner. Had the hostess been upset over the affair her agitation would have been communicated to the servants; and instead of one mishap there might have been several. A hostess should still "be mistress of herself tho China fall." In dinner-giving, as in life, it is the part of genius to turn disaster into advantage. "I was once at a dinner-party," said an accomplisht diner-out, "apparently of undertakers hired to mourn for the joints and birds in the dishes, when part of the ceiling fell. From that moment the guests were as merry as crickets."

Interrupting within the conversational group is perhaps the most insufferable of all impediments to rippling talk; and interruptions from without are quite as intolerable. What pleasure is there in conversation between two people, or among three or four, when the thought is interrupted every other remark? Frequent references to subjects entirely foreign to the topic under discussion give conversation much the same jerky, sputtering ineffectualness as sticking a spigot momentarily in a faucet prevents an even flow of water from a tank. People who have any feeling for really good conversation do not allow needless hindrances to destroy the continuity and joy of their intercourse with friends and acquaintances. And people who do permit these interruptions are not conversationalists; they are mere drivelers.

CHAPTER VII

POWER OF FITNESS, TACT, AND NICETY IN BUSINESS WORDS

There is an aspect of business words which has to do with social tact. "The social tact of business words" sounds incongruous on first thought. Business is largely force, to be sure; but a pleasing mien is often powerful where force would fail. Training in social instinct and nicety is more essential to a man's commercial interests than is visible on the face of things. For instance:

Customer (entering store)—"I wish a tin of 'Cobra' boot polish, black."

Dealer—"Sorry, madam, we do not stock 'Cobra,' as we are seldom asked for it. Do you wish polish for the class of shoes you are wearing?"

To tell a customer abruptly, "We do not carry such-and-such a brand in stock" has the effect of leading her immediately to turn to go. This is not cordial, nor gracious, nor diplomatic; hence it is unbusiness-like. Furthermore, to tell a customer that the brand she mentions is seldom asked for is immediately to question her judgment. The dealer, in this case, lost a chance to get attention on the part of his customer by failing to infer, the moment he mentioned her shoes, that she wore a good quality, had good taste, or common sense, or some such thing. His reply could have been vastly improved by an exercise of the social instinct. To answer her with some non-committal, tactful response would open up cordial relations at once and afford the chance easily and gracefully to lead the talk to another brand of polish.

Dealer—"Do you prefer 'Cobra' polish, madam? For high-grade shoes such as you wear we find this brand more generally serviceable and liked."

Telling expression, whether in business or in the drawing-room, depends as much upon how one says a thing as upon what one says; as much upon what one refrains from saying as upon what one does say.

What is the secret of the ability to put thought into tactful as well as vivid words? Or is there a secret? There are those who invariably say the right word in the right way. The question is: how have they found it possible to do this; how have they learned; how have they brought the faculty of expression to a perfected art? Or was this ability born in them? Or, if there is a secret of proficiency, do the adroit managers of words guard their secret carefully? And if so, why?

Piano artists, and violin artists, and canvas artists, and singing artists, are uniformly proud of the persevering practise by which they win success. Why should not ready writers and ready talkers be just as proud of honest endeavor? Are they so vain of the praise of "natural facility for expression" that they seldom acknowledge the steps of progression by which they falteringly but tenaciously climb the ladder of their attainment? A few great souls and masters of words have been very honest about the ways and means by which they became skilful phrase-builders. Robert Louis Stevenson, as perfect in his talk as in his written expression, said of himself: "Tho considered an idler at school, I was always busy on my own private ends, which was to learn to use words. I kept two books in my pocket, one to read, one to write in. As I walked my mind was busy fitting what I saw with appropriate words. As I sat by the roadside a penny version book would be in my hand, to note down the features of the scene. Thus I lived with words. And what I thus wrote was written consciously for practise. I had vowed that I would learn to write; it was a proficiency that tempted me, and I practised to acquire it. I worked in other ways also; often accompanied my walks with dialogs and often exercised myself in writing down conversations from memory. This was excellent, no doubt; but there was perhaps more profit, as there was certainly more effort, in my secret labors at home.[B] That is the way to learn expression. It was so Keats learned, and there was never a finer temperament for literature than Keats's; it was so, if we could trace it out, that all men have learned."

What, then, is the essential training necessary to the nice handling of words? The idea is quite general that an extensive vocabulary alone makes thought flow exactly off the tip of one's tongue or pen. But is this true? One should have a command of words, to be sure; one should know more descriptive words than "awful, fierce, fine, charming"—terms used in an unthinking way by people who do not concern themselves with specific adjectives. But to know how to use a vocabulary is of even more importance than to possess one. Indeed, merely to possess a vocabulary without the ability to weave the words into accurate, characterized designs on an effective background is ruinous to the success of any talker or writer. To employ an extensive vocabulary riotously is worse than to own none.

When the poet Keats wrote those well-known lines,

> "A thing of beauty is a joy forever
> Its loveliness increases,"

the first line stood originally:

> "A thing of beauty is a constant joy."

The poet knew that this was the thought he wanted, but he felt that it had not the simple, virile swing he coveted. And so the line remained for many months, "A thing of beauty is a constant joy," in spite of the author's many attempted phrasings to improve it. Finally the simple word "forever" came to him, "A thing of beauty is a joy forever." Then he had it, and he knew he had it—the essential note, the exact word. Certainly the word "forever" was a part of Keats's vocabulary; he undoubtedly knew this simple word. It was not the word, but adroitness in using it, which made Keats's lines complete in their polished and natural perfection.

One of the world's worshiped piano virtuosi, who has quite as intellectual a comprehension of words as of music, was asked by the editor of a magazine to contribute biographical data and photographs for an article on musical composers. The pianiste had published no compositions, and the gracious answer swung readily into line: "If your article is to deal exclusively with musical composers, I cannot be included. I have never published any of my compositions because I feel that they cannot add anything to my reputation as a pianiste, of which I am———" Just here, as with Keats's line, vocabulary could not serve the purpose. The pianiste could have said "of which I am proud." No, a modest phrase must express honest pride—"my reputation as a pianiste which I guard sedulously," or "defend zealously." No, this the exactness and simplicity of true art rejected. Then came the simple, perfect phrasing—"my reputation as a pianiste, of which I am somewhat jealous."

Unquestionably, as with Keats's word "forever," the word "jealous" was perfectly familiar. It was not any one exceptional word which was necessary, but a weaving of simple words—if I may be permitted the expression. Here, in order to get the effect desired this master-mind refrained from using a vocabulary. Words came readily enough; but the tongue was in command of silence because pretentious words failed the end. This perfection of expression is not a matter of vocabulary alone. It is more than vocabulary; it is a grappling after the really subtle and intellectual elements of the art of expression and persuasion.

Of what use all the delicately tinted tapestry threads in the world, spread out before a tapestry-worker, if he does not possess the ability to weave them into faultless designs, employing his colors sparingly here, and lavishly there?

"One's tongue and pen should be in absolute command, whether for silence or attack," says Stevenson again; and, more than on any quality of force, business success depends upon that same nicety in the use of words which selects the tactful expression, the modest and simple phrase, in the drawing-room; the sort of nicety which is unobtrusive exactness and delicacy; an artistry which in no way labels itself skilful. But underneath all, the woof of the process is social skill—that skill which is the ability to go back to unadorned first principles with the dexterity of one who has acquired the power to do the simple thing perfectly by having mastered the entire gamut of the complex.

CHAPTER VIII

CONCLUSION

Good conversation, then, is like a well-played game of whist. Each has to give and take; each has to deal regularly round to all the players; to signal and respond to signals; to follow suit or to trump with pleasantry or jest. And neither you yourself, nor any other of the players, can win the game if even one refuses to be guided by its rules. It is the combination which effects what a single whist-playing genius could not accomplish. Good conversation, therefore, consists no more in the thing communicated than in the manner of communicating; no more than good whist consists entirely in playing the cards without recognizing even one of the rules of the game. One cannot talk well about either cabbages or kings with one whose attention wanders; with one who delivers a sustained soliloquy, or lecture, and calls it conversation; with one who refuses to enter into amicable discussion; or, when in, does nothing but contradict flatly; with one who makes abrupt transitions of thought every time he opens his mouth; with one, in short, who has never attempted to discover even a few of the thousand and one essential hindrances and aids to conversation. As David could not walk as well when sheathed in Saul's armor, so even nimble minds cannot do themselves justice when surrounded by people whose every utterance is demoralizing to any orderly and stimulating exchange of ideas.

> "For wit is like a rest
> Held up at tennis, which men do the best
> With the best players,"

said Sir Foppling Flutter; and few would refuse to admit that fortunate circumstances of companionship are as much a factor of good conversation as is native cleverness. Satisfactory conversation does not depend upon whether it is between those intellectually superior or inferior, or between strangers or acquaintances; but upon whether, mentally superior or inferior, known or unknown, each party to the conversation talks with due recognition of its first principles. There are, to be sure, different classes of talkers. There are those of the glory of the sun and others of the glory of the moon. It is easy enough to catch the note of the company in which one finds one's self; but the most entertaining and captivating person in the world is petrified when he can not put his finger on one confederate who understands the simplest mandates of his art, whether talking badinage or wisdom. Without intelligent listeners, the best talker is at sea; and any good conversationalist is defeated when he is the only member of a crowd of interrupters who scream each other down.

Conversation is essentially reciprocal, and when a good converser flings out his ball of thought he knows just how the ball should come back to him, and feels balked and defrauded if his partner is not even watching to catch it, much less showing any intention of tossing it back on precisely the right curve. "The habit of interruption," says Bagehot, "is a symptom of mental deficiency; it proceeds from not knowing what is going on in other people's minds." It is impossible for a good talker to talk to any advantage with a companion who does not concern himself in the least with anybody's mental processes—not even his own.

Given conversation which is marked by conformity to all its unwritten precepts, "Men and women then range themselves," says Henry Thomas Buckle, "into three classes or orders of intelligence. You can tell the lowest class by their habit of talking about nothing else but persons; the next by the fact that their habit is always to talk about things; the highest by their preference for the discussion of ideas." Discussion is the most delightful of all conversation, if the company are *up to it*; it is the highest type of talk, but suited only to the highest type of individuals. Therefore, a person who in one circle might observe a prudent silence may in another very properly be the chief talker. Highly bred and cultured people have attained a certain unity of type, and are interested in the same sort of conversation. "Talk depends so wholly on our company," says Stevenson. "We should like to introduce Falstaff and Mercutio, or Falstaff and Sir Toby; but Falstaff in talk with Cordelia seems even painful. Most of us, by the Protean quality of man, can talk to some degree with all; but the true talk that strikes out all the slumbering best of us comes only with the peculiar brethren of our spirits.... And hence, I suppose, it is that good talk most commonly arises among friends. Talk is, indeed, both the scene and the instrument of friendship."

On the whole, then, the very best social intercourse is possible only when there is equality. Hazlitt in one of his delightful essays has said that, "In general, wit shines only by reflection. You must take your cue from your company—must rise as they rise, and sink as they fall. You must see that your good things, your knowing allusions, are not flung away, like the pearls in the adage. What a check it is to be asked a foolish question; to find that the first principles are not understood! You are thrown on your back immediately; the conversation is stopt like a country-dance by those who do not know the figure. But when a set of adepts, of *illuminati*, get about a question, it is worth while to hear them talk."

If we are to have a rising generation of good talkers, by our own choice and deliberate aim social intercourse should be freed from the barbarisms which so often hamper it. Conversation at its highest is the most delightful of intellectual stimulants; at its lowest the most deadening to intellect. Better be as silent as a deaf-mute than to indulge carelessly in imperturbable glibness which impedes rather than encourages good conversation. Really clever people dislike to compete in a race with talkers who rarely speak from the abundance of their hearts and often from the emptiness of their heads. On the other hand, one can easily imagine a sage like Emerson the victim of conceited prigs, listening to their vapid conversational performances, and can readily understand why he considered conversation between two congenial souls the only really good talk.

Marked conversational powers are in some measure natural and in some acquired; "and to maintain," says Mr. Mahaffy, "that they depend entirely upon natural gifts is one of the commonest and most widely-spread popular errors.... It is based on the mistake that art is opposed to nature; that natural means *merely* what is spontaneous and unprepared, and artistic what is *manifestly* studied and artificial.... Ask any child of five or six years old, anywhere over Europe, to draw you the figure of a man, and it will always produce very much the same kind of thing. You might therefore assert that this was the *natural* way for a child to draw a man, and yet how remote from nature it is. If one or two children out of a thousand made a fair attempt, you would attribute this either to special genius or special training

—and why? because the child had really approached nature." Just as a child, either with talent for drawing or without it, can draw a better picture of a man after he has been trained, than before, so can those not endowed by nature with ready speech polish and amend their natural defects. Neither need there be artificiality or affectation in talk that is consciously cultivated; no more indeed than it is affectation to eat with a fork because one knows that it is preferable to eating with a knife.

The faculty of talking is too seldom regarded in the light of a talent to be polished and variously improved. It is so freely employed in all sorts of trivialities that, like the dyer's hand, it becomes subdued to that it works in. Canon Ainger has declared positively that "Conversation might be improved if only people would take pains and have a few lessons." Nearly two hundred years before Canon Ainger came to this decision, Dean Swift contended that "Conversation might be reduced to perfection; for here we are only to avoid a multitude of errors, which, altho a matter of some difficulty, may be in every man's power. Therefore it seems that the truest way to understand conversation is to know the faults and errors to which it is subject, and from thence every man to form maxims to himself whereby it may be regulated, because it requires few talents to which most men are not born, or at least may not acquire, without any great genius or study. For nature has left every man a capacity for being agreeable, tho not of shining in company; and there are hundreds of people sufficiently qualified for both, who, by a very few faults that they might correct in half an hour, are not so much as tolerable." It is recorded of Lady Blessington by Lord Lennox in his *Drafts on My Memory* that in youth she did not give any promise of the charms for which she was afterwards so conspicuous, and which, in the first half of the nineteenth century, made Gore House in London famous for its hospitality. A marriage at an early age to a man subject to hereditary insanity was terminated by her husband's sudden death, and in 1818 she married the Earl of Blessington. Everything goes to prove that, in those few years during her first husband's life, she set herself earnestly to cultivating charm of manner and the art of conversation.

Talking well is given so little serious consideration that the average person, when he probes even slightly into the art, is as surprized as was Molière's *bourgeois gentilhomme* upon discovering that he had spoken prose for forty years. Plato says: "Whosoever seeketh must know that which he seeketh for in a general notion, else how shall he know it when he hath found it?" And if what I write on this subject enables readers to know for what they seek in good conversation, even in abstract fashion, I shall be grateful. When all people cultivate the art of conversation as assiduously as the notably good talkers of the world have done, there will be a general feast of reason and flow of soul; each will then say to the other, in Milton's words,

"With thee conversing, I forget all time."

www.ingramcontent.com/pod-product-compliance
Lightning Source LLC
Chambersburg PA
CBHW081733100526
44591CB00016B/2603